PLANNING FOR A NEW BOARDING SENIOR SECONDARY SCHOOL

in Jonglei Province, Southern Sudan

by
MECAK AJANG ALAAK

Submitted in partial fulfilment of the requirements for the Diploma in Educational Administration of the University of Leeds, 1980.

The ideas and opinions in this book are ultimately those of the author. Their authenticity is the responsibility of the author, not Africa World Books.

The publisher wishes to acknowledge and thank Dr Douglas H. Johnson for his invaluable help and support for Africa World Books and its mission of preserving and promoting African cultural and literary traditions and history. Dr Johnson and fellow historians have been instrumental in ensuring that African people remain connected to their past and their identity. Africa World Books is proud to carry on this mission.

© Mecak Ajang Alaak, 2022, All rights reserved.

© Cover photo by Abraham Mabior Rioc Manyang

ISBN: 978-0-6456127-8-3

No part of this publication may be reproduced, stored in a retrieval system, or transmitted, in any form, or by any means, electronic, mechanical, photocopying, recording or otherwise, without the prior permission of the publishers.

This book is sold subject to the conditions that it shall not, by way of trade or otherwise, be lent, re-sold, hired out or otherwise circulated without the publisher's prior consent in any form of binding or cover other than in which it is published and without a similar condition including the condition being imposed on the subsequent purchaser.

Cover design, typesetting and layout: Africa World Books
Unit 3, 57 Frobisher St, Osborne Park, WA 6017
P.O. Box 1106 Osborne Park, WA 6916

Acknowledgement

I would like to express my thanks to Mr. J. Glover, Director, Overseas Education Unit, University of Leeds, for his help and encouragement in the plan of the essay. My gratitude is due to him for painstaking assistance and unfailing patience in the course of going through the essay. I am indebted to him especially for the useful remarks and suggestion, and above all his motivating teaching was invaluable. My gratitude goes also to Dr. B. Garvey for his help in the technical production of this essay and his contribution in the course of educational administration. I am indebted to the British Council for providing me with financial assistance and thus enabling me to come to Leeds University to undertake this course.

Mecak Ajang Alaak
March, 1980
University Of Leeds, UK

CONTENTS

Introduction   9

Chapter One: Educational Background In The Province
Background Information About Jonglei Province   11
Historical Background of Education   16
The Present Educational System in Jonglei Province   18

Chapter Two: Location And Planning The School
The Objectives of a Boarding Senior Secondary School in Jonglei Province   27
The School Site   29
School Statistics   33
The School Construction Plans   36

Chapter Three: Administration and Organisation
General Administrative Function   38
The School Administration   41
The Teaching Staff and their Duties   44

Chapter Four: The Academic Work of the School
  Curriculum   46
  Examinations   50
  Inspections   52

Chapter Five: Enrolment And Discipline
  Enrolment   55
  Student Activities   58
  Discipline   60

Chapter Six: Financial And Administrative Control
  Finance   64
  Supplies and Equipment   67
  School Records   70

Chapter Seven: Summary and Conclusion   74

Appendices:
  Appendix A: Distribution of Schools in the Sudan by Provinces - Academic, Year 1977/78   79
  Appendix B: Distribution of Teachers in the Sudan by Provinces — Academic Year 1977/78   81
  Appendix C: Distribution of Pupils in the Sudan by Provinces - Academic year 1977/78 60   83
  Appendix D: School Facilities (Construction Plans): The Areas to be Occupied by Buildings in Square Metres   85

Bibliography   89
About The Author   93
Review   95

List Of Maps Diagrams And Tables

Maps:

Map I: Sketch Map of the Sudan Showing the Location of Jonglei Province	13
Map II: Sketch Map showing the Six Districts of Jonglei Province in the Southern Sudan	14

Diagrams:

Diagram I: The Educational System in Sudan	21
Diagram II: The Administrative Arrangement of the Regional Ministry of Education	42
Diagram III: How the School Administration will be Organized	47

Tables:

Table I: Pupil Enrolment in Jonglei Province by Level, Grade and Sex 1977/78 Academic Year	22
Table II: Primary School Enrolment as a % of Population Aged 7-12 and 7 years in Jonglei Province 1977/78	23
Table III: Number of Teaching Staff in Jonglei Province by District, Training, Sex and Language Ability	25
Table IV: Student Enrolment, Malek Senior Secondary School, by Junior Secondary School, 1979/80 Academic Year	31
Table V: School Administrative and General Staff	34

Table VI: Number of Lessons per Week in the Subjects to be offered   49
Table Vll: Student Enrolment During the School Construction Period   56

INTRODUCTION

The purpose of this paper is concerned with the plan for a boarding senior secondary school in Jonglei province, Southern Sudan. There is little educational documentation about this province and chapter one deals with background information: the geography, the people and the historical background of education. Lack of proper statistical data makes this plan to be "a plan without statistics". Most of the information is from my knowledge and my background experience as a schoolmaster and as a school administrator. Chapter two discusses the location, objectives, advantages and strategy of the boarding senior secondary school as the first of its kind in the province.

Chapter three deals with administration and organisation of the school and the relationship with the

Regional Ministry of Education in Southern Sudan. Chapter four talks about the school academic work and how the curriculum's weaknesses and deficiencies could be improved without the school contradicting the national educational policies. Chapter five gives proposals on student enrolment during the construction period, the student activities to be encouraged and how to improve student discipline. The last part of the paper deals with the financial management of the school, how the headmaster with his staff will control the school property and the maintenance of school records.

CHAPTER ONE
EDUCATIONAL BACKGROUND IN THE PROVINCE

Background Information About Jonglei Province

Until Sudan became independent in 1956, the Southern Sudan consisted of three provinces: Upper Nile, Bahr El Ghazal and Equatoria. In 1976, the three provinces were redivided to make six provinces. Upper Nile province was divided into two, the northern part remained as Upper Nile Province and the southern part became Jonglei Province (see map I page 13). Jonglei Province is divided into six administrative units called the districts (see map II page 14) Fangak, Waat, Akobo, Pibor, Kongor and Bor. There are four tribal groups in the province: the Nuers, the Dinkas, the

Anuaks and the Murles. The Nuers are mostly found in the Fangak District, Waat District and part of Akobo District. The Dinkas are found in Kongor District and Bor District. The Anuaks are found in Akobo and Pibor Districts. The Murles are found in Pibor District. Most of these tribes are nomadic people who centre their cultures and occupations on raising of Cattle.

Most of the Jonglei province falls in the flood zone, an area characterised by a lack of slope in the lay of the land, heavy impermeable soils and comparatively heavy rainfall of between 750 to 1,000 mm during a season of 6 to 7 months. The soil is insufficiently drained due to the lack of good natural drainage system. The area is susceptible to heavy flooding and water-logging. (1) According to the nature of flooding, the zone can be subdivided into four main areas:

a. <u>Highlands</u>: These are the higher areas which remain slightly above flood water level during the rainy season. They have more permeable soils and, due to steeper slopes, better drainage. These isolated islands with long ridges are formed on alluvial banks of rivers and water-courses. They act as refuge for the tribal people and their animals.

b. <u>Intermediate Land</u>: These lands are flat, low lying plains, subject to severe flooding or at least water-logging during the rains and almost waterless during the dry seasons. The intermediate land is so called because it lies at an intermediate level between the highlands and the 'toich' land, and it is the area of what is known as 'creeping flow' of the river water.

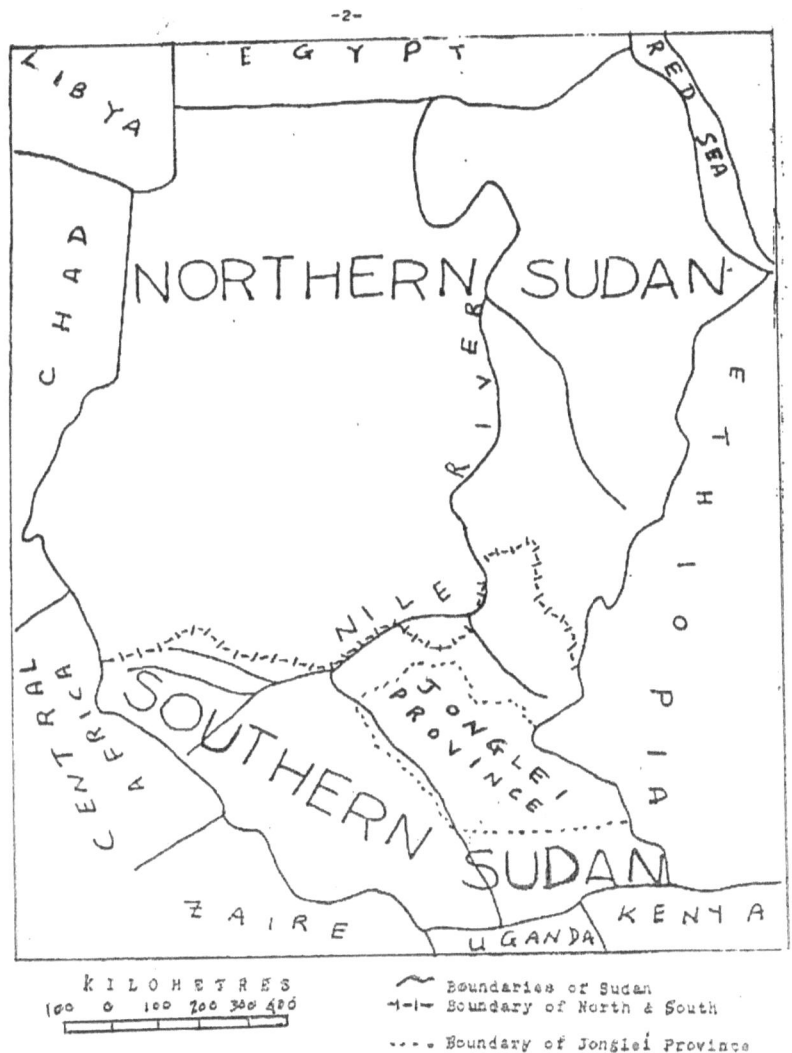

Map 1: Sketch Map of the Sudan Showing the Location of Jonglei Province

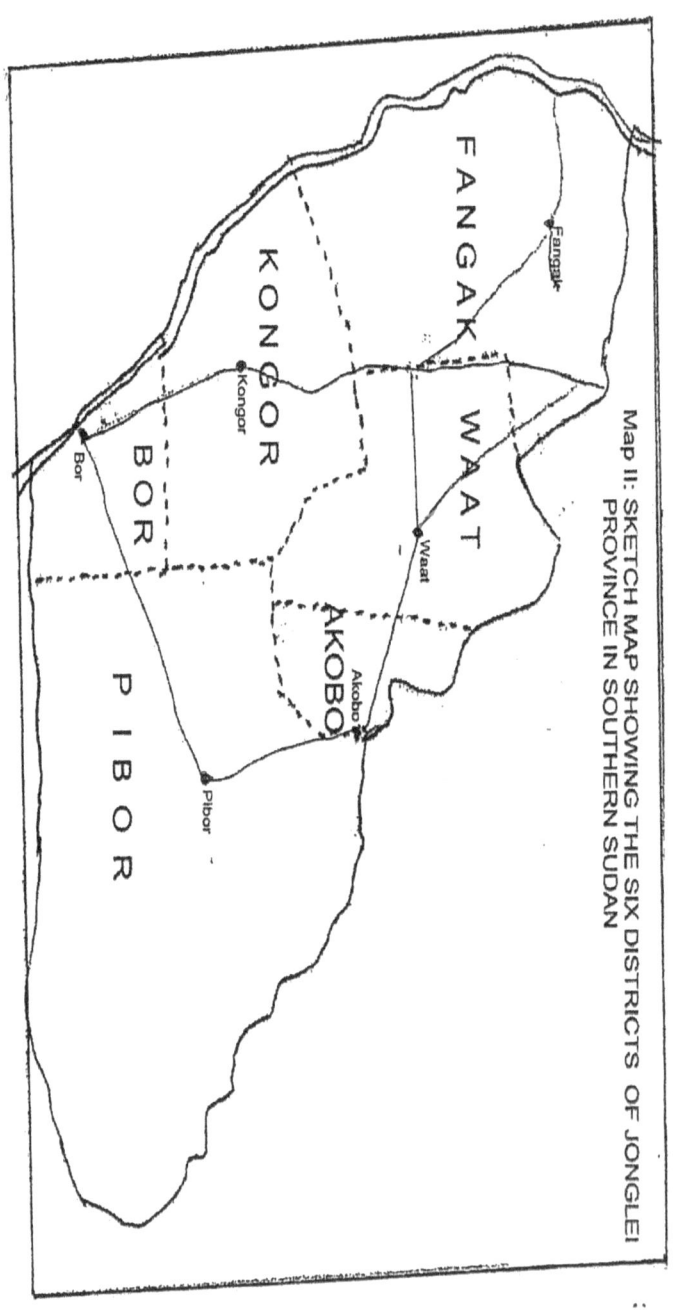

c. <u>Toich' Land</u>: These are areas divided by many rivers and watercourses. They are seasonally flooded by spill water from these rivers and water-courses. There is sufficient moisture throughout the dry season to support active grass growth.
d. <u>Sudd Land</u>: This area consists of land which is permanently below the level of the 'toich' land and therefore tends to consist of permanent and semi-permanent swamps. Vegetation in the sub-zone is predominantly papyrus.

This type of ecology and the climatic conditions make transportation and communication difficult in Jonglei Province. They have also resulted in the poor economic, social and educational development of the province. The colonial administration in the Sudan planned for a canal to drain the Sudd region and to save Nile waters which largely evaporate in the swamp lands. Anne Charnock writes of "the Jonglei Canal impact study, financed by the European Development Funds, a canal project (2) planned by the British over 80 years ago." The canal project was planned to bring development to the area. The French who took the contract are using a huge bucket wheel machine to dig the canal. On the 22nd October, 1979 BBC TV showed a film about the Jonglei Canal and life in the Province, "The lost waters of the Nile", by Alex Nisbett. This programme highlighted the importance of drainage and communication in the province.

Historical Background of Education

Education was introduced in the Southern Sudan for the first time by Christian missionaries during the Condominium (1898 — 1955). The Roman Mission and the Church Missionary Society divided the South into spheres of mission development. Gordon Hewitt writes, "The principal centres of Roman Mission in the 1920s were Lul and Tonga among the Shilluk Lord Cromer had laid down 'spheres' for mission development in the Southern Sudan before the Church Missionary Society (CMS) began work there in 1905." (3)

The missionaries received no cooperation from the tribal people of the South. The Southerners were rebellious to the outsiders at this time because some of their brothers were taken by the slave raiders. Beshir writes, "In the Southern Sudan, no less than twenty rebellions by Southern tribes, including the Nuers and Dinkas, took place between 1900 and 1919."(4)

According to the spheres system, the area which is now Jonglei province was assigned to the Church Missionary Society. In the province education started when a group of six missionaries from the Church Missionary Society (CMS) established a Mission and a school at Malek a few miles away from Bor (the headquarters of the province now) in 1906. This group of missionaries went back to England and in 1908; only Archibald Shaw returned to Malek. Gordon Hewitt writes,

> *"Of the six members of the pioneer party of 1906 only one was at work there two years later — Archibald Shaw. Shaw returned from furlough in October 1908 to Malek, on the right bank of the Nile eleven miles south of Government post at Bor. He brought with him a missionary recruit, W. H. Scamell. The mission station consisted of a large corrugated iron bungalow with four rooms on iron Girders; and some African huts The school and services were held on the veranda of the bungalow."* (5)

In 1936, there were only two mission schools in the province, the next mission school was opened on the Zeraf Island in Fangak District. Hewitt writes, "In January 1936, a second Nuer station was opened by the McDonalds at Juaibor on Zeraf Island." (6)

In 1956 Sudan got independence and Arabic was introduced in all the schools in the Southern Sudan. During the military government of General Aboud (1958 — 1964) the relationship between the South and the North suddenly deteriorated. In 1964 all the mission schools were taken over by the Government and the missionaries were expelled from the South. In all the schools in the South, the machinery of Government and the provision of Government services including education came to a standstill. When all the schools were closed down the people went to the bush or the neighbouring countries.

After the ratification of the Addis Ababa Accord the Regional Government of the Southern Sudan was established in March, 1972 and entrusted with the responsibility of provision, control and administration of primary, secondary and teacher-training education within the overall national educational policy.

The Present Educational System in Jonglei Province

According to the Local Government Act of the Democratic Republic of the Sudan the province is entrusted with the responsibility of provision of educational services and control of primary and junior secondary school levels within the regional and the overall national educational plans. The other two levels of education, namely the senior secondary school and the teaching-training levels, are responsibilities of the Regional Government in Juba. The head of educational authority in the province is the Assistant Commissioner of Education. He is the chairman of the planning Board of education in the province Executive Council Planning Board. He is the direct technical adviser to the Commissioner (the highest political authority in the province) of the province on education.

The educational system being followed in Jonglei Province is the general educational system in the Sudan. Diagram I shows the educational system in the Sudan: six years of primary education, three years of junior

secondary education and three years of academic senior secondary school, or four years of technical secondary school. In the province and in the Sudan as a whole, children start schooling at the age of seven. The ages for schooling are as follows:
- Primary education: 7 to 12 years;
- Junior secondary education: 13 to 15 years;
- Senior secondary education: 16 to 18 (or 19) years.

It must also be admitted that many pupils in Jonglei Province still commence schooling late. In 1977/78, academic year approximately was 7,059 pupils were enrolled in the primary school in the Jonglei Province. Table l, page 22 shows this enrolment by level, grade and sex. The percentage is less than the national and regional percentages. According to Ministry sources, "In the most recent school year (1975-76) approximately 97,000 children were enrolled in the government-maintained primary schools in the Southern Sudan Region. This number represents slightly less than 22% of the total primary school age population (i.e. all children 7 — 12 years of age in the region). This percentage (22%) compares with an average enrolment exceeding 50% in the rest of the country." (7)

Of the total number of 7,059 pupils enrolled in the primary schools in the province, girls constituted 851 (Table l) which is only 12%. The Regional percentage of girls in the primary schools is 25% (Total number of pupils was 106, 831 and girls were 26, 708). This presents imbalance is caused by the traditional idea that a woman is only the cook of the family. Another factor is that most of the primary schools opened in the rural areas are single sex schools. There are primary schools for girls in the main townships and the parents are not ready to allow their daughters to go and stay in the town even with near relatives. The widening gap between educations of the two sexes is a question on which the educational planners and decision-makers of the province and the Region should focus their attention.

Provincial authorities assume the responsibility for the salaries of the junior secondary school teachers. The province is also responsible for the upkeep of the school buildings and the supply of the school equipment. The language of instruction in the junior secondary schools is Arabic but English is taught as a subject. In the province there are six junior secondary schools in which in 1977/78 academic year there were 915 pupils enrolled. Of this number only 122 (13%) were girls (Table 1, page 22). Admission to the junior secondary school is by examination which is given in the final year of the primary school. Most of the junior secondary schools in the province are boarding because the schools are few and have to serve more villages in different areas.

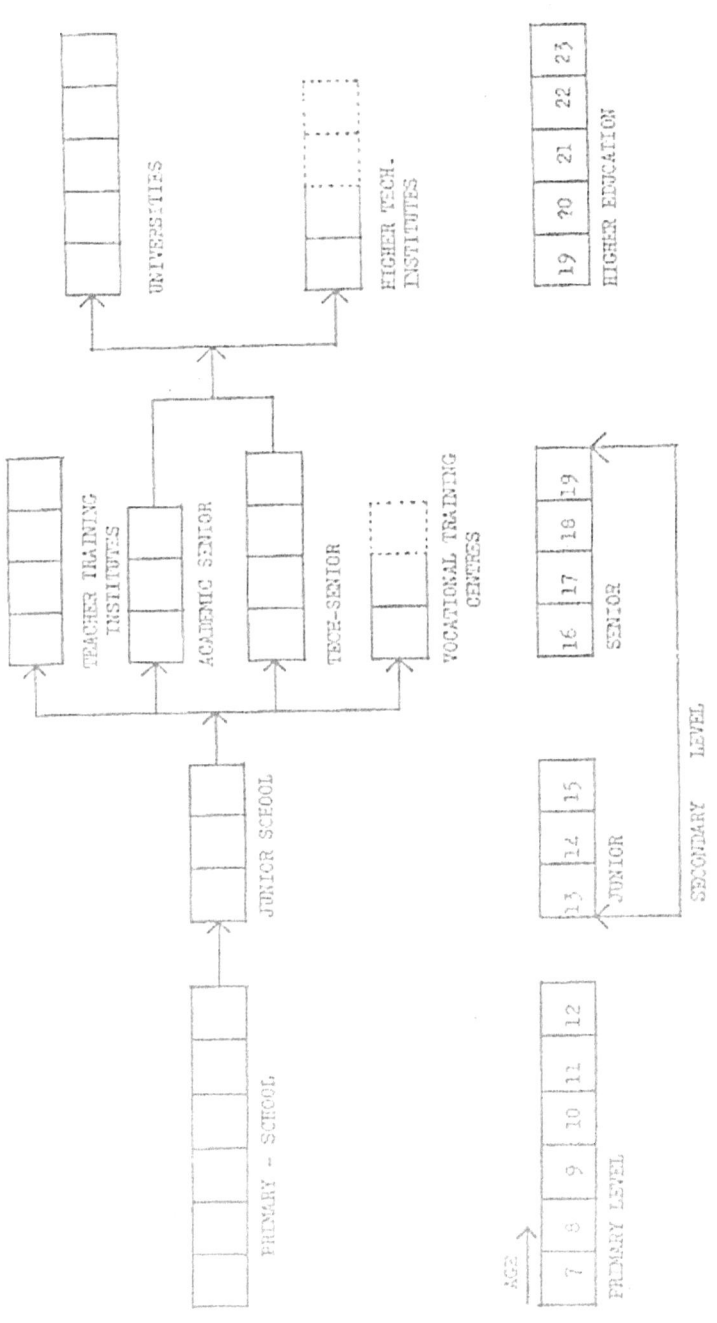

DIAGRAM 1: THE EDUCATIONAL SYSTEM IN THE SUDAN

Table 1: Pupil Enrolment in Jonglei Province by Level, Grade and Sex 1977/78 Academic Year

Level	Class	Male	Female	Total	% of Girls
Primary	P1	1931	281	2212	12.7%
	P2	1624	193	1817	10.6%
	P3	1046	121	1167	10.3%
	P4	687	98	785	12.4%
	P5	537	81	618	13%
	P6	383	77	460	16.7%
	TOTAL	6208	851	7059	12%
Junior	J1	312	52	364	14.2%
	J2	271	53	324	16.3%
	J3	210	17	227	7.4%
	TOTAL	793	122	915	13.3%

(Source: Educational Statistics in the Southern Sudan 1977-78, Part III: Jonglei p.5 and p.22).

Table II: Primary School Enrolment as a % of Population Aged 7-12 and 7 years in Jonglei Province 1977/78

District	Estimated 7-12 yr. pop.	% 7-12 yr. pop. P.1-p.6	Estimated 7 yr. pop.	% 7 yr. In. P I
Bor / Kongor	25, 158	15.6	5,198	22.3
Pibor	2,237	26.4	486	34.8
Waat / Akobo	9,114	17.7	1,961	25.9
Fangak	20,581	5.3	3,874	9.7
TOTAL	57,090	12.4	11,519	19.2

(Source: Education Statistics in the Southern Sudan 1977-78 Part I l l : Jonglei Province P. 8) Population estimates are projected from 1973 census. The district Bor/Kongor and Waat/Akobo have been combined as 1973 census regions were different to administrative districts. Population estimates projected from 1973 census.

Jonglei province has the least number of schools, teachers and students compared with any other province in the whole of Sudan. Appendices A, B and C shows the distribution of schools, teachers and pupils by provinces for the academic year 1977/78. That year there were 185 teachers (Table Ill) in primary schools in Jonglei Province. In this number only 8 (4.3%) were female teachers. Out of the primary teaching force about 75 (40%) were untrained. In the same academic year of 1977/78, there were only 40 teachers in junior secondary schools, and out of this number, females were 2 (5%). Table Ill shows that 31 teachers at the junior secondary schools (which is about 77.5%) are untrained. The demand for primary and secondary school teachers in the Province is very large but the supply is low. One of the reasons for this is that at present there do not exist any primary teachers training institutes or junior secondary school teachers institutes.

The historical background regarding education in the province and the conditions prevailing in the primary and junior secondary schools have been examined. It is perhaps appropriate to mention here that in Jonglei Province, there does not exist any senior secondary school neither of academic, technical or teacher training type as mentioned above. Because of the high demand for senior secondary education in the province; and the political pressure from the voters and the taxpayers, the Government was forced to make a decision. The Government announced that it would open an academic senior secondary school at Malek in 1978/79 academic year. The school was not opened that year, however 100 students have been enrolled in 1979/80 academic year.

Table III: Number of Teaching Staff in Jonglei Province by District, Training, Sex and Language Ability

Primary Level:

District	Trained			Untrained			Language Ability			
	M	F	T	M	F	T	Arab.	Eng.	Both	Total
Akobo	8	-	8	6	-	6	-	-	14	14
Bor	38	7	45	40	-	40	68	16	1	85
Fangak	28	-	28	5	1	6	27	-	7	34
Kongor	12	-	12	16	-	16	1	1	26	28
Pibor	8	-	8	4	-	4	-	-	12	12
Waat	9	-	9	3	-	3	12	-	-	12
Total	103	7	110	74	1	75	108	17	60	185

Junior Secondary School Level:

District	Trained			Untrained			Language Ability			
	M	F	T	M	F	T	Arab.	Eng.	Both	Total
Akobo	1	-	1	6	-	6	-	2	5	7
Bor	3	2	5	10	-	10	8	4	3	15
Fangak	1	-	1	4	-	4	1	-	4	5
Kongor	2	-	2	7	-	7	7	2	-	9
Pibor	-	-	-	4	-	4	-	-	4	4
Waat	-	-	-	-	-	-	-	-	-	-
Total	7	2	9	31	-	31	16	8	16	40

(Source: Educational Statistics in the Southern Sudan 1977-78 Part III : Jonglei Province, p. 9 and p. 16)

Note: 'Language ability' means the ability to present lessons in the language (Arabic or English).

Because the school has not yet been built at Malek, the school opened temporarily in November 1979 at Bor Junior Secondary School. The task for this paper in the following chapters is to plan for this boarding academic senior secondary school, both for physical development and curriculum development.

References

1. Regional Ministry of Finance and Economic Planning 1977. Southern Region, *The Six-year Plan of Economic and Social Development 1977/78-1982/83 (Nairobi: D.L. Patel Press (K) Ltd.)* P. 6.
2. Chernock, A. 1979 *"Assessing Sudan Canal's Impact on Tribal Tradition"* in New Civil Engine-el, 31 May 1979 P. 36-37.
3. Hewitt, G. 1971 *A History of the Church Missionary Society 1910-1943* (London: SCM Press Ltd.) p. 323.
4. Beshir M.O. 1969 *Educational Development in the Sudan 1898 to 1956* (Oxford: Clarendon Press) p. 24.
5. Hewitt, G. 1971 p. 332.
6. Ibid., p. 342.
7. *Regional Ministry of Education 197, Education in the Southern Sudan* (University of Durham) p. 30.

CHAPTER TWO
LOCATING AND PLANNING THE SCHOOL

The Objectives of a Boarding Senior Secondary School in Jonglei Province

We can see from the previous chapter that educational development in Jonglei Province lags far behind that of the other provinces in the Sudan. The only and the first senior secondary school was opened in November 1979 in the premises of Bor Junior Secondary School which lacks both space and comfort. The solution to this will be a new site which could be planned and developed accordingly.

One of the questions people are asking is why plan for a boarding senior secondary school? While many countries are discouraging such developments. It is true that boarding school is expensive and a country like the Southern Sudan may not be able to shoulder the cost. Accommodation and feeding will have to be provided. Extra work will have to be imposed on the limited number of staff to keep order during the free hours. But boarding education is unavoidable at this level, a school like this will have to serve a wide catchment area because there are no means of transportation as mentioned in the previous chapter. One of the advantages of a boarding school is that it will bring the youth together thus contributing to the unity and the general understanding of the different tribal cultures of the province.

The objectives of a senior secondary school in Jonglei province could be summed up as follows: Universal primary education is vital for the province and apart from general education pertaining to the senior secondary school the graduates of the school could work as teachers in the primary level. The secondary school facilities available will be used for the community of the provinces. The school will have the facilities to offer in-service training and retraining to the teachers of the province.

The presence of a senior secondary school will add to the civic pride of the province and will give opportunity to people of older age to study in the evening or on vacation (summer) courses. The school will undertake the specific tasks of organising the students and the community for employments essential for the transformation of the environment of the province. This undertaking could be an answer to the Jonglei Canal's impact on the tribal traditions of the people. There is a great demand for senior secondary school education by the students of the junior secondary school. This demand is increasing since the standards of certain families are improving. According to Poignant, the economic improvement and the rise in family living standards create new material and psychological conditions which demand better education. (1)

The School Site

When planning or locating a school, the planner should have in mind the national education objectives and strategy. In the Southern Sudan some of the objectives and strategies for development of education are as follows: provision and equitable distribution of educational opportunities to all the communities especially those in the rural areas; maximum decentralization of educational planning and implementation of projects through participation of citizens in their local councils in planning education and enabling local councils to run all educational institutions themselves. Some of the basic factors for the school site are given by Castaldi:

> *"The characteristics of school sites depend upon many factors, including the type of school proposed for the site, its initial and projected ultimate enrolment, the breadth of educational programme, the cost of*

availability of the sites, the grade levels to be housed, and the aesthetic values possessed by the community. The specific characteristics and general location of the school sites needed in the future should be clearly stated and discussed in the rationale supporting the site programme. " (2)

The taking of a decision on statistical data could also be considered. For the academic year 1977/78 the primary and junior secondary school statistics in the province shows that Bor District has the highest numbers. (3) Let us look at statistics of the enrolment of Malek Senior Secondary school for the academic year 1979/80 which was 100 pupils. The enrolled pupils were mainly from three junior secondary schools in the province (Bor, Kongor and Akobo).

Table IV: Student Enrolment, Malek Senior Secondary School, by Junior Secondary School, 1979/80 Academic Year

Junior Secondary School	No. of Students
Bor Junior Secondary School	49
Kongor	26
Akobo	16
Others*	09
Total	100

Source: Examination results 1979.
*The other 9 students are citizens of the province who completed their junior secondary in other provinces.

In the senior secondary school a curriculum for rural education should be introduced so that pupils are enabled to practice crop production, gardening, animal husbandry, poultry-keeping, local crafts, etc. It is obvious from these subjects that this type of curriculum will help the pupils to link their education to the local need and environment. This is the way to help pupils to learn practical work. It will also make the school economically self-supporting. This will help to show the local population that education can contribute to local development. Having these factors in mind the planner for the school site should consider the availability of enough fertile agricultural and with good water supply.

The cost factor is an important influence upon the school location. In setting up and maintaining educational institutions one should utilise to the maximum the self-help potential of the communities. The site of the school should be where building materials are available or to which they could easily be transported. The local community should consider private boarding and weekday boarding schemes as means of removing responsibility for boarding children from the school to their parents.

After the government announced the establishment of a senior secondary school in Jonglei province, consideration was given to all relevant factors to determine the site. The factors, of which some are mentioned above, are the structure of the school system in the Southern Region and in Jonglei Province, the distribution of supplies by the province, fertile agricultural land, good water supply, cost function, population in a catchment area and last but not least, the name of the school. The site proposed and approved was Malek in Bor District. Malek is only eleven miles away from Bor Town on the Bor-Juba road on the river Nile. The road between Bor and Juba is one of the all-weather roads In the Southern Sudan, so that supplies and services could easily be extended to Malek either by land or by river. One of the main reasons why Malek was chosen was because of its historical background. It was the first mission station opened in the Southern Sudan in 1906 as mentioned in chapter one.

School Statistics

The government policy on the establishment of a boarding senior secondary school, which is unavoidable at this level, is that it should be developed as a four-stream school with full complement of 600 pupils in twelve classes. This is thought to be optimum size for this type of school in terms of economy and efficiency. The term "stream" is understood in the Southern Sudan to mean the number of classes in each grade or in each age group. Also the term "comprehensive" is understood to mean a school with very wide curricula. In England most of the secondary schools are comprehensive and such schools use mixed-ability teaching. Pupils are admitted without any test of ability or aptitude and the pupils are not streamed. When planning school facilities the educational planner should first know the school statistics. The school is going to be a three grade school with four streams of 100% boarding with a class unit of 50 pupils: that is 600 pupils in total. This is according to the Government policy as mentioned.

Table V: School Administrative and General Staff

a) Administrative Staff

PARTICULARS	NO.
Headmaster	1
Deputy Headmaster for Administration	1
Deputy Headmaster for Academic Affairs	1
Bursar	1
Head Clerk	1
Store-keeper	1
Senior Book-Keeper	1
Clerk	1
First Class typist (Arabic and English)	2
Medical Assistant	1
Laboratory Assistant (Chemistry, Physics, Biology)	3
Librarian Assistant	1
TOTAL	15

b) Teaching Staff

SUBJECT	NO.
Mathematics	5
English	5
Arabic	4
Physics	3
Chemistry	3
Biology	3
Geography	3

History	3
French	2
Religious Education	2
Physical Education	1
Arts and Crafts	1
Possible Part Time Agriculture Teacher	1
TOTAL	36

c) Non-Teaching Staff

PARTICULARS	NO.
Plant Attendants	2
Head Driver	1
Drivers	4
Head Carpenter	1
Carpenters	6
Head Cook	1
Cooks	6
Time-Keeper	1
Electrician	1
Electrical Apprentices	4
Plumber	1
Head Builder	1
Builders	9
Librarians	3
Head Labourer	1
Labourers	10
Roneo Operator	1
Gardeners	5
Watchmen	5

Messengers	3
Conservancy Men	4
Kitchen Hands	4
Shepherd	3
Water Carriers	3
TOTAL	80

The School Construction Plans

Since the school is going to be in a rural area all the pupils, members of the staff and the school labour force will have to be accommodated within the school premises. This page gives the land required and the area to be occupied by buildings is given in appendix D. In the Southern Sudan there is enough land which is already Government property. The unit of measurement commonly used is the 'feddan'. One 'feddan' is the area of a rectangular plot of land 60 metres by 70 metres (i.e. one 'feddan' is 4,200 square metres). The land required would be distributed as follows:

Buildings	8 feddans
Physical/Recreational Activities	4 feddans
Agriculture and Farming Land	480 feddans
Future Expansions	44 feddans
TOTAL	536 feddans

Approximately the land required would be 2,251,200 square metres and if we want the land to be square in shape it would be a square of 1.5 kilometres by 1.5 kilometres.

Approximately this plot of land would be 556 acres (100 square metres = 0.0247 acres). From appendix D we could see that the total area to be occupied by building is 12,145 square metres. The cost per square metre for a building in Juba (capital city of Southern Sudan) is LS. 110 (one hundred and ten Sudanese pounds). We could add the additional cost of 20% for inflation and transportation of materials to the school site.

The cost for the buildings 12,145 x 110 = LS 1,335, 950
20% transportation and inflation - LS 267 190
TOTAL = LS 1 603 140

Chapter six will discuss the school financial management and how to obtain the funds for the construction of the school.

References

1. Poignant, R. 1974 *The Relation of Educational Plans to Economic and Social Planning* (Paris: Unesco/IIEP) p. 36.
2. Castaldi, B. 1969 *Creative Planning of Educational Facilities* (U.S.A.: Rand McNally and Company) p. 62.
3. Regional Ministry of Education 1978. *Educational Statistics in the Southern Sudan*
4. 1977-78 part I l l : *Jonglei Province* (juba: Ministry of Education) p. 5 and p. 12.

CHAPTER THREE
ADMINISTRATION AND ORGANISATION

General Administrative Function

When planning for a new senior secondary school which is going to be the first of its kind in the province, one should look at the administration and management which form an important part of the educational planning process. The main task here is planning for the process of senior secondary educational development in Jonglei Province with the aim of making it more effective and efficient in responding to the needs of the pupils and society. By this process we will be able to make use of the resources we have to achieve the secondary education we want. At present, the Regional Ministry of Education directs, controls, and manages senior secondary schools as regards planning, coordination and overall supervision. In the Southern Sudan the highest decision-making body is the Regional Government Cabinet known as the High Executive council: the Regional Minister of Education is a member of the council.

The administrative head of the Regional Ministry of Education is the Director who is the highest civil servant in the Ministry. The Ministry is divided into four divisions responsible for the overall management, servicing and monitoring of education in the Region. The four divisions are as shown in diagram II (i) Administration (ii) Planning (iii) Inspection and (iv) Technical Services. Each division is headed by a deputy director. The Ministry has three boards in which the administrative decisions are taken, namely Planning Board, Scholarship Board and the Examination Board. Diagram II shows the administrative arrangement of the Regional Ministry of Education.

The duties of the Director of the Regional Ministry are as follows: He/She is the administrative head of the organisation, the chairman of all the three boards mentioned above, the technical advisor to the Minister and he follows up executive decisions and directives of the organisation. The Deputy Director for the administration helps and acts in the absence of the Director, assists the Director in the office's management in the day to day action, follows and directs all the assignments made in the organisation and is responsible for finance.

The Deputy Directory for planning has the sole responsibility for the planning and execution of the projects and programmes, and is also responsible for research, budgeting and statistical analysis. The Deputy Director for professional matters is responsible for efficient supply of professional and material resources, and directly supervises the smooth running of the general examinations. The Deputy Director for inspection is responsible for guidance, coordination of educational activities, and consultancy services and teacher education programmes.

I would define the educational management system in the Southern Sudan as largely centralized; it is bureaucratic, slow-moving and wasteful of time and resources. This problem was realised and it is now the policy of the Government of Democratic Republic of the Sudan to decentralize the administration of education in the interests of efficiency and democratisation. This policy has not yet been adopted in the Southern Sudan. One of the priorities in the objectives and strategies for educational development in the Southern Sudan that could be recommended is maximum decentralization of administrative system and of educational planning and implementation of educational projects for the following reasons.

Programming and monitoring the approved plans (i.e. reviewing, evaluating, revising and modifying) could be done without such complicated bureaucratic procedures. The desirable policy and direction could be done with the participation of the local population thus avoiding any blame on the side of the Government from the people. The collection, classification and analysis of the statistical data could be done within a short distance. The senior secondary schools will also exercise a degree of autonomy in the field of decisionmaking.

The Assistant Commissioner for Education in the province is not directly involved in the administration of a senior secondary school even though he is the head of the unit. Help is still needed from him by the headmaster whenever there is a problem of accommodation or lodging in the school. In the school decision-making the option of other educational administrators, teachers of various levels, parents and the community is voiced in an organisation known as the Teachers and Parents Council which is one of the branches of the only political organisation in the country — the Sudanese Socialist Union (SSU). This body may cause an inspection to be made of any educational establishment in the province by officers appointed by the organisation.

The School Administration

The administrative head of a senior secondary school in the Southern Sudan is known as the director. In England he is known as the headmaster, principal, headteacher or just the "head". The word principal is commonly used in the United States of America. In this paper the word headmaster will be used except when making a quotation. The headmaster would be appointed by the Regional Ministry of Education. He should be either a deputy headmaster, head of the department or a senior teacher in one of the senior secondary schools.

Diagram II: The Administrative Arrangement of the Regional Ministry of Education

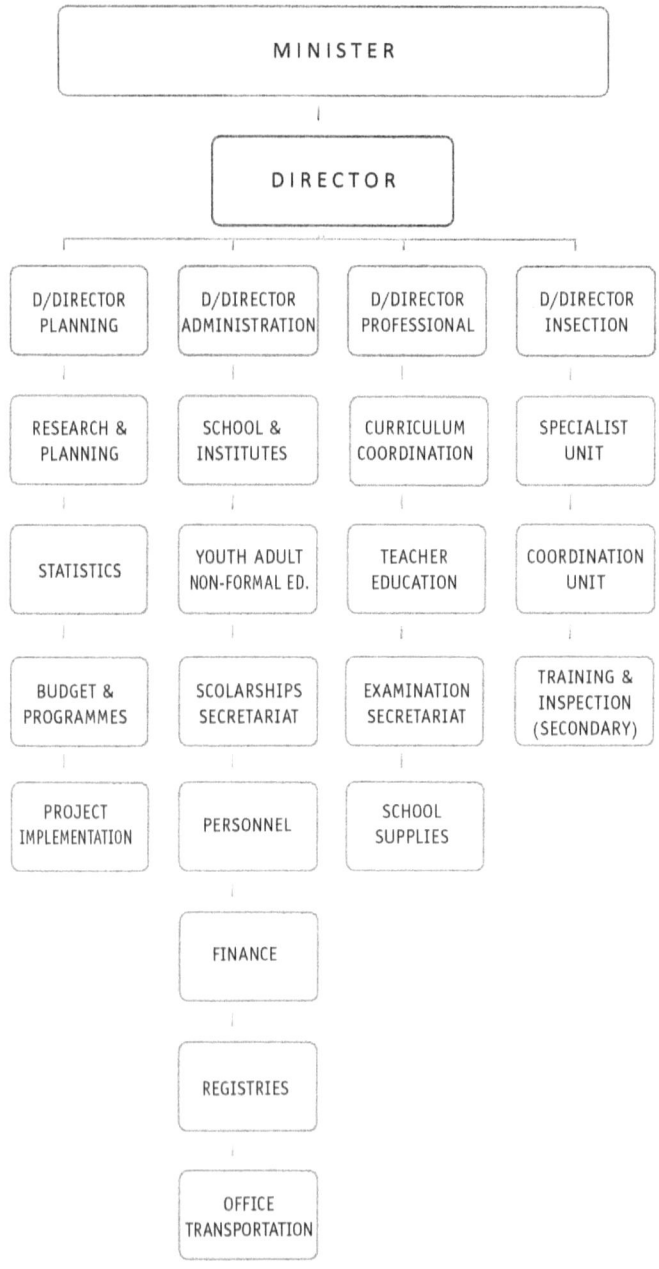

Teachers within the province are normally given preference in filling a headmaster's position. He should be a recognized educational leader who could direct and supervise his staff. He should be able to gain the confidence and cooperation of the local community. Stanley W. Williams in his book, "Educational Administration in Secondary Schools" says,

> *"Citizens' groups and educational circles have long recognized that those individuals who held secondary school administrative positions have been chosen largely because of their educational ability, experience, and training. As a result, the principal is accepted in the community as expert in the fields of school organization and administration, instructional leadership, school law and finance, as well as in many other specialized areas." (1)*

The headmaster will be assisted by two deputies: deputy headmaster for administration, deputy headmaster for academic affairs. He will also be assisted by two non-teaching staff: the school bursar who will be responsible for finance and the headclerk who is the headmaster's secretary. All the above four officials will have to be appointed by the Regional Ministry of Education or they may be transferred from other senior secondary schools. Diagram II shows how the school administration will be organized.

The Teaching Staff and their Duties

The number of teaching staff needed has been given in chapter two. The teachers will normally be appointed by the Regional Ministry of Education and will be subject to transfer at any time. Most of the general transfers are made during the vacation.

Each departmental subject will be headed by head of the department who will be a senior teacher to be appointed by the headmaster in consultation with his two deputies.

Members of staff will be assigned different responsibilities. Some will be housemasters and others will be classmasters. The housemasters will be responsible for the accommodation and other social problems of the students. They will be assisted by the headprefects and the houseprefects. These headprefects and houseprefects will be pupils elected by the pupils in their dormitories who will be given responsibility for keeping order. Classmasters will be responsible for academic problems of the students. They will have to follow the students' progress and evaluate each student's academic achievement. The classmasters will be assisted by classmonitors who will be students elected and given authority over their fellows in their classes.

Effective communications, which are methods of instructing, passing and receiving information, are essential if the school is to function smoothly. The headmaster will have to communicate through the deputies, head of departments, housemasters, and classmasters or in a general meeting. Young teachers who are new and without defined areas of responsibility would be reminded that they have a responsibility to the head of department as a subject teacher. The headmaster must trust his staff with responsibility and support decisions made by them. Communication in a school is very important and all the members of staff, students and ancillary staff will have to understand it. The school will also communicate with the Regional Ministry of Education, provincial authorities, and local education authorities, junior secondary schools in the provinces and the universities in the country. The school will also communicate with the parents and the community in general.

In this chapter we have been looking at the general administrative system of the Regional Ministry of Education and how the internal administration of the school would be organized. Our next concern must be to examine the school academic work. How will the curriculum and the educational development programmes of the school be adapted to the provincial needs? Consideration will also be given to the examination system and to the school inspection.

Reference

1. Williams, S.W. 1964 *Educational Administration in Secondary Schools* (U.S.A: Holt, Rinehart and Winston, Inc.) p. 29.

CHAPTER FOUR
THE ACADEMIC WORK OF THE SCHOOL

Curriculum

Senior Secondary schools in the Southern Sudan consist of three types of establishments: senior academic secondary schools, senior technical secondary schools and senior commercial secondary schools. The present aims of the Government is diversification of senior secondary school education, and achievement of a balance between academic education on the one hand and technical and vocational training on the other. The percentage ratio is envisaged as 60% and 40% respectively. It is also a policy of the Government to establish each type of senior secondary school separately. As mentioned in the first chapter the school being planned

Diagram III:
How the School Administration will be Organized

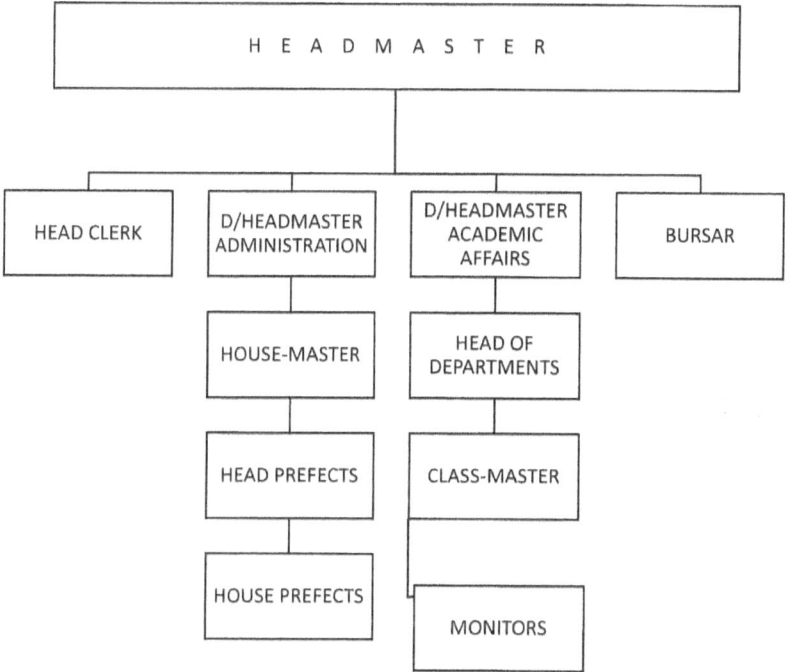

in this paper is an academic senior secondary school, therefore we are going to consider the curriculum for the academic school only.

The curriculum is the central nerve of the educational system through which the educational objectives flow; where it is not planned well, the teacher is like a man thrown in the middle of the River Nile who does not know how to swim. The curriculum thus is vital for the future of our youth who are the fathers and leaders of tomorrow of Jonglei Province. The school will provide for the pupils an improved and strengthened education. This could be done through adjusting to educational changes without alteration in the culture of the community and the society. Since we can only assess zero secondary school education in the past, it would give us a better ground on which to plan, consolidate and assess for the future. The objectives of this planned school will arise from careful consideration, and analytical and realistic look at the entire educational system in terms of the present needs and the future conditions of our province, Sudan, Africa and the world at large to which we should contribute as responsible members.

The subjects of instruction will vary considerably in their capacity to contribute to the following objectives to develop pupils' education: aesthetic, physical, linguistic, mathematical, ethical, scientific, social and personal. Table VI shows the number of lessons per week in the subjects to be offered.

Table VI: Number of Lessons per Week in the Subjects to be offered

SUBJECTS	NO. OF PERIODS PER WEEK
English	6
Mathematics	8
Arabic	4
Physics	3
Chemistry	3
Biology	3
Geography	3
History	3
French	3
Religious Knowledge	2
Physical Education	3
Arts and Crafts	2
TOTAL	42

All the syllabuses will have to be coordinated to ensure balance and avoid repetition and overlapping in related subjects like History and Geography, Mathematics and physics. The teachers will be encouraged to include imaginative and stimulating teaching methods so as to encourage a proper understanding of syllabus concepts. In the first year the subjects Physics, Chemistry and Biology will be taught as General Science. There will be seven periods daily Monday to Saturday and each period will be 45 minutes. Since all the students and teachers will be living on the campus, the school will start at seven in the morning and end at two in the afternoon. The school will have an Academic Board to be headed by the Deputy Headmaster for Academic Affairs. One of the functions of this Academic Boards will be the need to create new subjects (e.g. agriculture, local languages in the province, etc.) and review the curriculum balance within the limits of the teaching staff, part-time teachers or the availability of proper qualified staff. Afternoons will be free and could be used for extra subjects which will be practical in nature and will also be used for sports. The students will be organized in groups according to their dormitories headed by the housemasters and assisted by the houseprefects.

Examinations

The purpose of examination in the Southern Sudan is a calculated selection, made in a way designed to filter out students of the same ability who could be allocated in groups and who could cope with the academic senior secondary school studies. The school is going to continue with this policy for some time because there will not be enough places available for all the students. The school will use examinations as one of the means by which the school can measure the extent of the changes described above.

We will be able to investigate if the changes occur because of the activities planned by the school.

C.A. Anderson in his book, "The Social Context of Educational Planning", said,

> *"Strict examination standards and close articulation among levels of schools on the basis of those examinations (i.e. selection) will raise the correlations. Yet, at the same time, a highly selective school system relying upon academic examinations may diminish the total influence of the school upon individuals' lives, and it will diminish the aggregate effect of schools upon economic growth." (1)*

It is clear from the viewpoint of the writer that examinations narrow students' fields of study, they do not study subjects that lead to occupational goals which are needed by a developing country like the Southern Sudan.

The main objective of this academic senior secondary school will be the preparation of the students for the Sudan Examination Certificate, an examination which gives the passport to enter any university in the country. Students in the first year will be divided by random selection into four equal classes because they will be of the same ability range. These classes will follow the same syllabus and receive the same kind of teaching using the same methodology.

In the second and third year which is the final year, the students will be selected into examination-oriented objectives because they will have to choose some subjects. According to policy in the Sudan Examination

Certificate, the students will take the four compulsory subjects: Mathematics, Arabic, English and Religious Knowledge (Islamic or Christianity). In addition they will have to choose either three or four subjects according to their interests developed and encouraged during the three years in the school. Those with ability for sciences will have to choose from the following subjects: Additional Mathematics, Physics, Chemistry and Biology. Those who wish to prepare for humanities will choose from the following subjects: Geography, History, General Science, Arts and Crafts and French.

Inspection

The school inspectorate system is organized and administered in the Regional Ministry of Education Headquarters. Teachers, Inspectors and supervisors are all members of the teaching profession: their common responsibility is to promote and improve education. The inspectors and supervisors will be of great help to the school; they will suggest factors influencing teachers' morale, professional knowledge and competence, sense of vocation and devotion to duty. Inspectors will always be highly welcome to the school. The school will regards inspectors and supervisors as friendly helpers and objective advisers, not as spies and potential informers as thought by other schools before. The headmaster will have immediate personal knowledge of the school and children; the inspector will bring wide experience and can compare one school with another.

The school will have internal inspection, as the headmaster and the two deputies will have to evaluate for future development. They will have to assume more responsibility for the standards and progress of the school. The heads of the department will have to inspect and supervise the work of the teachers in their departments. The deputy headmaster for academic affairs will have the overall academic supervision. The deputy headmaster for administration will also have a general overall supervision of the school property and equipment.

Inspection is useful because inspectors will check and report in the public interest. They are concerned with efficiency and improvement, not only in maintaining but raising educational standards.

F.J. Goodwin pointed this out when he said,

> *"I should perhaps give my views in the matter of formal general inspections. I think they have a useful and, indeed, necessary part to play in the life of a school. In my own experience — and I am speaking of the visitation which has come upon me as well as that I have asked for — I have found general inspections terrifying in prospect. But the results of these thorough assessments by outside experts I have nearly always considered very useful and, often, inspiring. In fact general inspections are like vaccination, unpleasant to anticipate, uncomfortable to undergo but very beneficial in results."* (2)

According to what has been quoted above the school will make the full use of inspection as well as inspection reports, because of the following reasons: the report will help the school administration and management to adjust according to the desired direction. The heads of the departments and class teachers will find new ideas and suggestions. The reports will also help all the teachers to adjust their work to the need of their classes. The school will cooperate with the specialists unit of the division of inspectorate in producing teaching materials for the school. This will help the school financially since the books which will be used by the school will be brought from outside the country and will be very expensive.

The school will coordinate training courses for the staff with the inspectorate.

In this chapter we have been considering the role of the inspectors and the supervisors in connection with the curriculum and the supervision of the school work. In chapter five we will look at the student's enrolment, student activities and student discipline and the role of the supervisor in connection with the student counselling and guidance programmes.

References

1. Anderson, C.A. 1974 *The Social Context of Educational Planning* (Paris: UNESCO/IIEP) p. 27.
2. Goodwin, F.J. 1968 *The Art of the Headmaster* (London: Cox and Wymen) p. 208.

CHAPTER FIVE
ENROLMENT AND DISCIPLINE

Enrolment

The school construction program will have to continue in the same phase with the student enrolment so that the facilities available could be utilized properly. It is planned that the school will continue to function in Bor Junior Secondary School for the first two years and will move to the new site by 1981/82 academic year when there will be only nine streams with 450 students. Table VII shows student enrolment planned for the construction period. The school construction will be completed by the year 1984 when the school will be in full swing with twelve streams.

Table VII: Student Enrolment During the School Construction Period

CLASSES	1979/80	1980/81	1981/82	1982/83	1983/84
1st Year	100	150	200	200	200
2nd Year		100	150	200	200
3rd Year			100	150	200
TOTAL	100	250	450	550	600

The students who have finished junior secondary school in the province and have passed the Senior Secondary School Entrance Examination will be admitted according to the Government policy as mentioned earlier.

In Jonglei province there has been no consideration about the education of girls as far as senior secondary education is concerned. This is because they are segregated educationally. The school will have to consider the possibility of allowing girls to study with boys. This must be done because according to the culture of the people of the province there is no sex segregation; the boys and girls mix and go to the cattle camp together but there are no serious problems. If the school is co-educational, then the province will be considering the next senior secondary to be a technical or commercial senior secondary school but not academic for girls. This will be cheaper for the province because it will avoid the duplication of staff and buildings. The dormitories for the accommodation of girls will have to be separated from the others. Positive and realistic guidance should be planned for these girls and a good matron should be appointed as member of the staff.

From my experience in the past about the dates of the re-opening of the senior secondary schools, there was no fixed academic school calendar and there were wide discrepancies. Late arrival of teachers and students at the school has been common even one month after the opening date. The school academic calendar will be fixed and teachers should be in the school one week before the official opening date and no student will be allowed to register two weeks after this date. The academic school calendar should be fixed and unified all over the country so that teachers coming from the Northern Sudan should have time for holidays. It is desirable that the school should use the following school calendar for 1980/81 academic year session:

Session 1980-1981

1st Term: Monday 14th July 1980
- Saturday 27th September 1980

2nd Term: Monday 13th October 1980
- Saturday 4th December 1980

3rd Term: Monday 5th January 1981
- Saturday 4th April 1981

Promotion examinations to other classes will be arranged one week before the end of the third term so that students are given their results. The same academic calendar should be used for the following years. The school will conduct an introductory orientation programme for the first week to acquaint the students with the school aims, objectives and philosophy. All the students will have to have student identity cards and the school badge for easy identification and differentiation.

Student Activities

The school will be a democratic society which will give fair consideration to pupils' opinions and suggestions. The school administration will encourage students' activities which will range from student council or student union, school club and school societies to extracurricular activities. This will be done by allowing students to organize themselves to have a student union which will be one of the means of communication with students. The student union aims should be compatible with the school's educational objectives and the union should operate on a democratic basis. The student union should help the students to understand the problems of the school and to develop responsibility and leadership. The goal of the student union should be to help and promote education to the community by giving writing and reading classes to those who did not have the chance of primary education.

The union should be aware of the areas of responsibility

in which it operates and should support itself financially from local contributions. The student union will have an appointed qualified staff adviser. The students will be allowed and encouraged to organize school societies with an interested member of the staff as an adviser or sponsor appointed by the school administration. The school will encourage the formation of the following societies or clubs: music society, agriculture society, cultural society, drama society, photographic society, geography society, history society, etc.

The school will have assembly programmes and each programme should be well planned by the assembly committee of teachers which should have student representatives. Many speakers from the community and outside should be invited for the assembly programme. The time of the assembly programme may not be during school working hours since all the students and staff will be living on the school campus. The programme of the assembly and student activities should be to instill in students the spirit of being a member of the group, loyal and respectful. The aims of the student activities should be according to what Williams said:

> "The activities found in the secondary school should provide for student growth in the areas of leadership, health, cooperation, exploration, social adjustment, and school and community service and should supplement the classroom instructional programme. Serious attempts should be made to attract students who lack

> *social and personal adjustment and who ordinarily would refrain from participating in the programme on a voluntary basis. Counsellors and teachers should seek out those individuals and encourage them to join an organization that should meet their needs and interests." (1)*

Athletics and sport will be encouraged since there will be enough playing grounds according to the school construction plans. Since it will be a boarding school there will be the advantage of using the afternoons for sports and athletics. The regional Ministry of Education should make the yearly schedule for athletics contests among schools so that there is no serious loss of classes. This could be planned so that contests can take place during the break between terms.

Discipline

The dictionary definition of the word discipline is, "training, especially of the mind and character, to produce self-control, habits of obedience." Sister Marie Phippipa defined discipline as:

> *"The word discipline has undergone some linguistic changes, yet basically the meaning is the same as always, and has to do with the 'discipline of those in the learning situation, who are placed in the care of a competent qualified person, with the authority to bring*

about conditions which enable learning to take place. This learning is concerned not only with acquiring knowledge of trade or profession, but with learning to become a whole person. Because of the need for control by recognized authority, discipline has acquired the additional meaning of being associated with well-drilled good order imposed by authority, carrying with it the notion of sanctions for violation of the code of rules." (2)

I am sure the school will not be free from disciplinary problems. The school surely will reflect the cultures, habits and attitudes of different tribes of the province. The school will also reflect the rural and the urban problems of the communities and if there is stealing, vandalism, dishonesty and violence the school is bound to inherit some of them. The children who will be admitted to the school were born and grew up during the seventeen year civil war in the Sudan and the war behaviour will be reflected. This behaviour has already been seen in the existing senior secondary schools in the Southern Sudan. There has been serious violence with physical attacks on members of one tribe by members of the other tribe within a school or physical attacks on individual students and even teachers. Some of the schools were closed down last year because of the student violence. In some schools there was indiscipline in the form of irritation to teachers in the classroom, disrespect for property and personality, indifferences to practical activities such as school sports and school clubs or societies, disorder in the dining hall and classrooms. This made things difficult for the school administration and on top of that a community or society cannot progressively exist if member lie, cheat and only think of themselves.

The causes of indiscipline in Southern Sudanese schools have their roots in the planning and administrative arrangements of the schools and the Regional Ministry of Education in Juba. Most of the schools have overcrowded classrooms so that the teachers find it difficult to locate the troublemakers; this also results in less effective teaching. Poorly equipped pupils enter the senior secondary school because they have not been given the proper basic education in the primary and junior secondary schools. It is also because the educational system of the country is heavily biased towards the learning and memorisation of factual knowledge with little or no relevance or applicability to everyday living and livelihood. The teachers are poor academically and untrained as shown at the beginning of this paper. In most of the schools there are not enough teachers and even when they are there they may not be in the schools for the first few weeks and the students begin to go about causing problems for others and for themselves. I would not hesitate to mention that selective examinations are also the cause of indiscipline in the schools. At the end of each academic year there are examinations which are meant for selecting students to the next classes for the following academic year. Since some of the students have been lingering without doing their studies, they begin to create big political problems thus stirring up strikes or demonstrations that could lead to the closure of the schools without examinations being taken.

In this chapter, we have been considering the student enrolment in relation to the school construction programme and student indiscipline which is one of the educational constraints in the Southern Sudan. In the next chapter, we will consider the financial problems of the school and how the students could be encouraged to grow food so that there could be a solution to the problem of the lack of green vegetables in the school.

Other problems like school supplies, equipment and records will be mentioned.

References

1. Williams, S.W. 1964 *Educational Administration in Secondary Schools* (USA: Holt, Rinehart and Winston, Inc.) p. 345.
2. Philippa, S.M. 1979 "Discipline: a Search for Meaning" Jennings, A. (ed.) *Discipline in Primary and Secondary School Today* (London: Latimer Trend and Company Ltd., Plymouth) p. 92.

CHAPTER SIX
FINANCIAL AND ADMINISTRATIVE CONTROL

Finance

One cannot really talk about planning a new senior secondary school without first considering how the funds could be obtained. The construction of the school needs money which must be provided by the Regional Government. The funds for supplies, equipment and food services must be presented in a budget to be approved by the Regional Assembly. The school was one of the projects that was proposed and was to be financed by the Central Ministry of Education in the development budget of 1978/79. It is worth noting that all of the development budget of 1978/79 for education in the whole country was cancelled because there were no funds. However, a development budget for 1979/80 was prepared for the Region and was to be allocated for this planned school in Jonglei Province. Many international multilateral, bilateral and voluntary organisations have the interest to improve the economic and social development of the Southern Sudan. This was shown at the time of rehabilitation and resettlement. Abu Dhabi has come out to finance this school in Jonglei Province and when the cost is known it will be communicated to them.

Jonglei province is rich in cattle and the people could be encouraged to contribute them to finance the school constructions. This was done in 1977 when they contributed thousands of cattle for the building of the new provincial headquarters in Bor. Since there is a vigorous cattle trade in the province there should be a tax on cattle brought to the market for sale. Production of local materials by the local population should also be encouraged for the school construction.

Since the headmaster is the school business manager, he/she must have a good knowledge of school finance. He must know all the financial legislation in relation to the senior secondary school finance. He must understand school budgeting, revenue and expenditure. The headmaster will be assisted by the school bursar who will be a welltrained accountant. The headmaster will receive the approved budget for the school at the beginning of each academic year. The budget will consist of three parts: chapter one known as personnel: these are the salaries and wages, chapter two known as Services: this amount will be for services which do not include salaries, e.g. water, fuel supplies and maintenance of equipment. The third part is the Development budget which will be used for construction of the school buildings or purchase of new furniture, books, laboratory equipment, art and home economics equipment.

The headmaster should be familiar with the procedures for making purchases. He should also know the salary scale for classified and unclassified staff. At the end of the school year the headmaster will start with the preparation of the new budget. The new budget will be presented to the Planning Board of the Ministry where the headmaster must be prepared to defend all items requested in the budget. When this budget is passed by the Regional Ministry of Education it is to be presented to the Regional Planning Board of which the Deputy Director for planning is a member. The school will ask the Regional Ministry of Finance through the Regional Ministry of Education to prepare a budget calendar that will indicate when various funds will be available so that there is no waste of time in following up; this will give more efficiency to the school as well as the Ministry.

In 1976/77 academic year a school fee of LS 16 (sixteen Sudanese pounds) was introduced in senior secondary schools as part of contribution to the pupil's feeding. These fees were abolished by the new Regional Government in 1978 and were substituted by what is known as educational tax. This tax was added on the existing tax, and then is now being paid by everybody even those who could not get places in the schools for their children. I believe that education is investment and the direct recipient should also pay a part of it. The educational tax is now being credited to the accounts of the Regional Ministry of Finance which is paid out some times for other purposes. This amount should be credited direct to the accounts of the Regional Ministry of Education for educational development and solving of educational emergency problems.

In 1979, it was noted with great concern by the headmasters of senior secondary schools that there were delays in arrival of salaries to the schools. This was thought to be mainly caused by the decision of the Regional Ministry of Finance that no payment of salaries would be effected unless on production of paysheets. It was also noted that sending of paysheets to Juba every month entails a lot of delay, more expenditure on the transportation of bursars and reduces the life of the vehicles since all the roads are rough. To solve this, the school will calculate the monthly salaries of the school and ask the Regional Ministry of Finance through the Regional Ministry of Education to send the same amount monthly to the account of the school with the bank branch in the province.

Supplies and Equipment

We have already seen in the last chapter that the students in the existing schools have no respect for the school property and equipment. You cannot decide to order furniture, books and equipment unless you know how to control and maintain them well. In the past students of senior secondary schools used to pay a deposit of five Sudanese pounds for any breakage to any of the school property.

It was discovered by the headmasters of the schools that students easily get away with very expensive textbooks only to lose the five pounds deposit. Hence, the school will increase the deposit to fifteen Sudanese pounds to discourage them from running away with expensive books. On top of this I would recommend the suggestion of Williams:

> *"Textbooks should be issued to teachers (not to students) by the textbook room. Textbook requisition blanks should be completed by the teacher, students should sign the box opposite the correct book number, and student identification should be made in the book in the event it is lost or mislaid... Textbooks returned by the teacher should be in numerical order and any losses or discrepancies should be noticed." (1)*

Students should be charged 150% price of any book lost. All the school property should be numbered: beds, chairs, desks mainly those that will be issued to the students. Whenever the students are going for holidays all the school property will be given back to the store before they will be allowed to go away. The deputy headmaster for administration will have the copy of the school inventories so that the storekeeper could also be checked at the end of each academic year. The school will send in the list of book supplies and equipment needed three months before the tender is advertised by the Regional Ministry of Education. The school will try to obtain the following teaching aids: tape and cassette recorders with cassettes, overhead projector with some acetate sheets and rolls, cinema projector, radio and television. Teachers will be encouraged to utilise the materials available in the local area, they should teach from the environment because the equipment mentioned above may be expensive and difficult to secure.

One of the causes of unrest in senior secondary schools in the Southern Sudan is the food service. Two months before the beginning of each academic year the feeding contracts are processed and signed by the Regional Ministry of Education for the supply of foods to schools. When the contractors are not paid on time there is sometimes no constant flow of food items to schools and this leads to shortage of foods. To solve this the school will first have a change in the curriculum. Agriculture will be introduced in the school and the land which is for agriculture will be divided up so that each student will be given a plot of land 50 metres by 50 metres. The school will ask for one or two agriculture tutors who will help the students to grow different crops and green vegetables which are now lacking in many schools. The students will sell the produce to the school at a reduced price. The tools and implements will be budgeted by the school and students will pay fees for using them. This amount will be used to replace the tools, implements and will also be used for the purchase of seeds.

The Regional Ministry of Education should make the school budget for feeding of students by calculating the amount spent on one student per day so that the school can know the limit of cost of each meal. The consumption of local feeds should be encouraged by the school, because they could be produced locally. There is no need to give the students bread when we do not grow wheat in the Southern Sudan. As mentioned in the first chapter, the people of the province centre their cultures and occupations on raising cattle. The school will have a dairy farm and each student will be encouraged to bring along one milking cow which will be kept in the school dairy farm to supplement the school diet. This will also help the student because he can sell part of the milk for cash which can buy other minor needs. One advantage for the cows that will be brought by students is that there will be veterinary care for them. At the end of the school academic year the student will be free to drive away his/her cow. The idea of 'using what we have to get what we want' should be encouraged even in the school construction. We should not rely on what we do not possess or produce locally.

School Records

The division of Education Planning, Research and follow-up in the Regional Ministry of Education sometimes finds it difficult to compile yearly statistics on education with a high degree of coverage and reliability because the schools do not have proper school records.

It will be our policy to have an accurate records system. The Regional Ministry of Education gave one of the objectives on senior secondary school as shown below:

> *"Both Curriculum and teaching need to be reformed to increase their relevance and effectiveness as means of training in knowledge, understanding, application, reasoning ability, creativeness, self-reliance, social consciousness, physical and aesthetic development. To achieve this type of liberal, all-round education, these schools need to be equipped with laboratories, libraries, art and craft facilities, and the requirements for drama, sports and physical education, horticulture and farming, and for girls needlework and home economics. Students should also be required to participate actively in the domestic duties of maintaining and caring for their schools and boarding premises." (2)*

To be able to work according to this policy, the school records must be able to help the teachers to guide the children to develop their talents and work. The students' records help the teachers to guide the children to choose a career and to participate in the national economic growth. The records help the school in sorting them out into many ability groups which could be taught according to their speed of learning. The student record could indicate the following: individual behaviour, leadership ability, sociability, honesty and others like working ability. The records also help the school headmaster to give a written report on a former student when it is requested as a reference by the Government employing agencies or business institutions. School records should be kept well because they will also be useful for long term references.

The school will always have the following statistical records: total enrolment giving the number of girls as well as the number of boys, students' ages and the student enrolment as a percentage of the population of the age group (16-18 years) in the school catchment area. Number of boarding and day students, pupil/class number, pupil/teacher ratio, number of students repeating, drop-outs, and the promotion rates. These records will be communicated to the Division of Educational Planning three weeks after the opening of the school. The school will have a duty report book which will be used by the duty master to record major discrepancies that are subject to correction. This will help the headmaster with his deputies to measure the success of the day to day smooth and efficient operation of the school and its programmes.

The headmaster will be assisted by the head clerk in maintaining accurate records for all the members of the staff. The records will have the teachers' qualifications and any additional training that might be required, his salary scale, length of service, date of appointment and the dates of promotions, positions held before and at present.

The maintenance of careful records will contribute to the smooth progress of the school. From records it will always be possible to verify the dates and what has been done in the past thus giving a continuous historical information about the school.

References

1. Williams, S.W. 1974 *Educational Administration in Secondarv Schools* (U.S.A.: Holt, Rinehart and Winston, Inc.) p. 444.
2. Regional Ministry of Education 1976 *Education in the Southern Sudan* (University of Durham) p.58.

CHAPTER SEVEN
SUMMARY AND CONCLUSION

There is no simple formula concerning planning a new senior secondary school which could be copied by all new schools in the developing countries. What makes them differ is the fact that the needs and conditions of each country are different and distinct from every other country. Our difficulties in Jonglei Province are the lack of funds and the lack of building materials for the construction of the school. When this school is established, it will answer some of the problems of our manpower needs. The outputs from this planned senior secondary school in the province will contribute to the education system as well as the economic growth of the province. The graduates of this school will be encouraged to join teaching so that they become the source of primary school teachers. This will help the province to overcome the limitations imposed by the manpower supply to the extent that enrolment of 30% of primary school age population from (7-12 years) is achieved by 1985/86. Plans should be made to train and upgrade some of them to teach in junior secondary schools in the province.

It is true that the schools in the Southern Sudan have a majority of the teachers untrained. The schools also have a great shortage of teachers. The introduction of parttime teachers in the schools should be a partial solution. In order to solve this problem compulsory national service in teaching should be introduced for all Southern Region citizens who graduate from universities and higher institutions.

It is recommended that one of the priorities in educational planning is to have a planning section in each province so that the collection, classification and analysis of statistical data could be done within a short distance. This will help the educational planners to obtain better statistical data which are a prerequisite to educational planning.

A co-educational system should be encouraged to avoid the duplication of staff and buildings in each school catchment area. Educational administration should be decentralized so that the school and local educational authorities could get more cooperation from the parents and community. At the moment education in the Southern Sudan is considered to be the sole responsibility of the Regional Ministry of Education.

The use of locally made materials should be encouraged by the school. Students will have to grow much of their own food, mainly green vegetables. They will also be asked to help as part of the labour force in contributing to self-help schemes for the construction of school buildings. This proposal is recommended because it will reduce the school development cost.

Lack of money is considered to be the major constraint on education development. I believe that poor administrative control of property, financial management and school plans are the real waste. It is my sincere hope that Jonglei Province, which has limited resources which it cannot afford to waste, will re-examine the question of property control and better administrative plans in her educational system. The situation in the Sudan is like the one to which Coombs refers:

> *"Money, however, was not only the bottleneck. At least three other kinds of shortage plagued educational development in the 1960's: (a) the limited administrative abilities of educational systems to plan and transform plans and money into desired results, (b) the long time required to recruit and develop competent staff for new schools, (c) the limited capacity of local construction industries."* (1)

The Curricula in the school and teaching methods should be developed and practically oriented and suited to the realities and requirements of the Southern Sudan in general and Jonglei Province in particular. It must equip the pupils with basic knowledge and skills necessary to enable them to live happier and healthier lives in the rural areas and contribute to the raising of living standards in the community.

Reference

1. Coombs, P.H. 1974 *What is Educational Planning?* (Paris: UNESCO/IIEP) p. 28.

APPENDIX A

Distribution of Schools in the Sudan by Provinces, Academic Year 1977/78

PROVINCE	PRIMARY	JUNIOR	SENIOR	TECHNICAL
Northern Province	335	115	13	1
Nile Province	400	153	14	3
Khartoum Province	447	155	31	12
El Gezira Province	932	291	37	6
White Nile Province	283	73	10	4
Blue Nile Province	335	65	7	—
Kassala Province	387	59	8	4

Red Sea Province	157	26	5	3
Northern Kordofan Province	365	86	8	2
Southern Kordofan Province	267	50	7	1
Northern Darfur Province	256	36	5	2
Southern Darfur Province	235	33	4	4
Jonglei Province	50	6	—	—
Upper Nile Province	107	20	4	1
Lakes Province	60	8	1	2
Bahr El Ghazal Province	127	17	2	1
Eastern Equatoria Province	202	20	2	1
Western Equatoria Province	96	6	—	2

(Source: Central Ministry of Education 1978 Educational Statistics Academic Year 1877, p.78)

APPENDIX B

Distribution of Teachers in the Sudan by Provinces Academic Year 1977/78

PROVINCE	PRIMARY	JUNIOR	SENIOR
Northern Province	2783	747	197
Nile Province	2725	880	236
Khartoum Province	3444	1536	780
El Gezira Province	6787	2464	826
White Nile Province	2309	663	210
Blue Nile Province	2158	538	118
Kassala Province	2707	488	196

Red Sea Province	1011	243	182
Northern Kordofan Province	2540	690	184
Southern Kordofan Province	1713	548	75
Northern Darfur Province	2039	523	105
Southern Darfur Province	1709	335	81
Jonglei Province	185	40	—
Upper Nile Province	518	149	61
Lakes Province	292	43	18
Bahr El Ghazal Province	615	72	15
Eastern Equatoria Province	843	427	36
Western Equatoria Province	411	74	12

(Source: Central Ministry of Education 1978 Educational Statistics Academic Year 1977/78)

APPENDIX C
Pupils in the Sudan by Provinces Academic Year 1977/78

PROVINCE	PRIMARY	JUNIOR	SENIOR	TECHNICAL
Northern Province	75677	18510	5586	219
Nile Province	97544	21428	6247	278
Khartoum Province	169394	37305	14283	2862
El Gezira Province	255529	53594	15506	1717
White Nile Province	76607	15085	5146	708
Blue Nile Province	79214	12211	2782	—
Kassala Province	94203	13294	3927	1055

Red Sea Province	30478	5660	2358	521
Northern Kordofan Province	78277	14425	4015	276
Southern Kordofan Province	64698	8989	2038	—
Northern Darfur Province	55225	6881	2461	239
Southern Darfur Province	52411	5929	1662	534
Jonglei Province	7059	1058	—	—
Upper Nile Province	20693	2796	1411	—
Lakes Province	8840	320	769	—
Bahr El Ghazal Province	19933	2090	463	200
Eastern Equatoria Province	46718	6528	849	200
Western Equatoria Province	18369	1459	—	—

(Source: Central Ministry of Education 1978 Educational Statistics Academic Year 1977/78)

APPENDIX D

School Facilities (Construction Plans): The Areas to be Occupied by Buildings in Square Metres

(i) School Administration

DESCRIPTION OF ITEMS	AREA IN SQUARE METRES	UNIT	TOTAL AREA
Office Headmaster	40	1	40
Deputy Headmaster for Administration	30	1	30
Deputy Headmaster for Academic Affairs	30	1	30
Bursar	30	1	30
Clerk	20	1	20
Maths Department	35	1	35
Arabic Department	35	1	35
English Department	35	1	35

Geography Department	35	1	35
Science Department	35	1	35
Staff Common Room	90	1	90
Other Departments	35	4	140
TOTAL			545

(ii) Academic

DESCRIPTION OF ITEMS	AREA IN SQUARE METRES	UNIT	TOTAL AREA
Class Rooms (50 pupils each)	60	12	720
Laboratories (Biology, Chemistry, Physics)	92	3	276
Art/Craft Room	110	1	110
Multipurpose Workshop	110	1	110
Store (Hardware-furniture)	60	1	60
Store (software - stationary- books)	60	1	60
Library	114	1	
Multipurpose Hall	300	1	300
Toilets Ablutions	10	7	70
TOTAL			1820

(iii) Boarding

DESCRIPTION OF ITEMS	AREA IN SQUARE METRES	UNIT	TOTAL AREA
Hostel for Students	360	8	2880
Student Common Room & Store	60	8	480
Toilets/Ablutions Student	60	8	480
Centre	100	1	100
Kitchen and 2 Stores	200	1	200
Dining Hall	200	1	200
One Store (Outside Kitchen)	100	1	100
Health Centre (10 Beds) Sick Bay	120	1	120
Student Co-operative Shop	120	1	120
TOTAL			4620

(iv) Staff Quarters

DESCRIPTION OF ITEMS	AREA IN SQUARE METRES	UNIT	TOTAL AREA
Senior Houses	120	8	960
Middle Standard Houses	110	12	1320
Junior Houses	86	10	860
Bachelors' Mess	400	2	800

Teachers' Centre	120	1	120
Teachers' Co-operative Shop	60	1	60
TOTAL			4120

(v) Labourers' Quarters

DESCRIPTION OF ITEMS	AREA IN SQUARE METRES	UNIT	TOTAL AREA
Labourer Houses (3 rms.)	50	8	400
Labourer Houses (2 rooms)	40	10	400
Jnr. Labourer Houses (1 rm.) Workers'	20	10	200
Co-operative Shop	40	1	40
TOTAL			1040

BIBLIOGRAPHY

Books:

Anderson, C.A. 1974 The Social Context of Educational Planning (Paris: UNESCO/IIEP)

Beshir, M.O. 1969 Educational Development in the Sudan 1898 to 1956 (Oxford: Clarendon)

Castaldi, B. 1969 Creative Planning of Educational Facilities (U.S.A.: Rand McNally and Company)

Central Ministry of Education 1978 Educational Statistics Academic Year 1977/78 (Khartoum)

Coombs, P.H. 1974 What is Educational Planning? (Paris: UNESCO/IIEP)

Curle, A. 1971 Educational Planning: the Adviser's Role (UNESCO/IIEP)

Goodwin, F.J. 1968 The Art of the Headmaster (London: Cox and Wyman Ltd.)

Hallak, J. 1977 Planning the Location of Schools (Paris: UNESCO/IIEP)

Harbison, F. 1974 Educational Planning and Human Resource Development (Paris: UNESCO/IIEP)

Hewitt, G. 1971 A History of the Church Missionary Society 1910-1943 (London: SCM Press Ltd.)

Mallison, V. 1977 Comparative Education (London: Heinemann)

Poignant, R. 1974 The Relationship of Educational Plans to Economic and Social Planning (Paris: UNESCO/IIEP)

Regional Ministry of Education 1976 Education in the Southern Sudan (University of Durham)

Regional Ministry of Education 1978 Educational Statistics in the Southern Sudan Part Ill: Jonglei Province 1977/78 (juba)

Regional Ministry of Finance and Economic Planning 1977 Southern Re ion the Six-year Plan of Economic and Social Development 1977/78 — 1982-83 (Nairobi: D.L. Patel Press (K) Ltd.)

Williams, S.W. 1964 Educational Administration in Secondary Schools (U.S.A.: Holt, Rinehart and Winston, Inc.)

Articles in Books:

Philippa, S.M. 1979 "Discipline: a Search for Meaning" Jennings, A. (ed.) Discipline in Primary and Secondary Schools (London: Latimer Trend and Company Ltd., Plymouth)

Articles in Journals:

Charnock, Anne 1979 "Assessing Sudan Canal's Impact on Tribal Tradition" New Civil Engineer, 31 May 1979

ABOUT THE AUTHOR

Mecak Ajang Alaak was born in 1944 in South Sudan. He attended Malek Primary School under Church Missionary Society, CMS, and Rumbek Secondary School. He later proceeded to the University of Liberia, where he studied and graduated with a double degree in Mathematics and Physics; and to the University of Leeds in UK where he obtained an advanced degree in Education Management. He also studied French at Lubumbashi University in the Democratic Republic of the Congo.

Mr. Alaak currently serves as the Chairperson of Jonglei State Electoral Commission. He was the founding director of the refugee schools in Ethiopia and Kakuma Refugee Camp, which served the educational needs of the "Lost Boys and Girls". His care for this special group of the refugees rightfully earned him the title of the "father of the Lost Boys". His memoir titled "the Father of the Lost boys" was recently written by his son, Yuot Ajang Alaak and published by Fremantle Press, Western Australia 2020. Before he became a refugee, he served in many capacities in the Sudanese Ministry of Education. He taught Mathematics and Physics at his Alma Mater of Rumbek Senior Secondary school before he became the founding principal of Malek Senior Secondary in Jonglei State. He served on the special committee which researched the area where Jonglei Canal was to be carried out. He also served as the director for Educational planning, Development and Scholarships for South Sudanese. Ajang was a member of the Board of Directors of the Australian Refugee Association, South Australia. He was also the former lay member of Anglican Church Synod of South Australia (1998-2005).

Mr. Alaak is a father and grandfather. At his young age, he was a great sportsman; he was a great wrestler among his Dinka peers and held a record in high jump (1.85 meters) in the African School Athletic Competition, which was organized in Addis Ababa in 1967.

REVIEW

Alaak, M. A. (1980). Planning for a new boarding senior secondary school in Jonglei province, Southern Sudan. The University of Leeds, pp. 1-97.

Alaak's case for building a boarding senior secondary school in Jonglei is a thoughtful, pragmatic, and visionary in terms of the problems to address and formulation of the curriculum. The building of the boarding senior secondary school would address the dearth of trained teachers across the province, and intellectuals who can engage with understanding and provide locally inspired expertise in the discussions around the construction of Jonglei Canal. The later reason is pertinent since the resumption of the canal is back in the limelight.

Though the eruption of wars did not ensure boarding school realize its objective of producing local intellectuals to engage in the discussion surrounding the construction of Jonglei Canal, divine works in mysterious ways. One of the key voices in the current discussions of Jonglei Canal is a son from Jonglei province, who perhaps could have benefited from the senior secondary school had it not been due to war. Secondly, Mr. Alaak ended up as a school planner and director of the schools in a refugee camp, where he perhaps planted the seed in the hearts and minds of so many young men, some of whom are intellectually endowed and are shaping the discussions around the resumption of Jonglei canal construction. What a prophecy!

Mr. Alaak has proposed a curriculum which realistically would incorporate the local communities' diversity in tribes and economic activities. The curriculum would secondly factor in the student profiles such as war experiences as well their learning needs and demands of 19th century. The secondary school as well as its curriculum focus would ensure all the students from various backgrounds are brought together to learn and appreciate their diversity, and perhaps develop a sense of nationalism as opposed to tribalism. Additionally, the curriculum would provide skills for the war traumatized children to transition into society. And finally, the curriculum was envisioned to raise awareness about, and modernize local economic activities such as pastoralism and agriculture.

It has been over 40 years since Mr. Alaak researched and wrote a plan for building the senior secondary school. The problems, however, he envisioned to solve are still dogging the young nation of South Sudan, and especially the greater Jonglei province. The tribes are more divided than ever, and constantly engaged in wars, which have caused loss of lives, displaced and traumatized individuals. Secondly, many local citizens still travel to neighboring countries to seek secondary school education since there are no qualified, trained teachers. Additionally, the local communities have relegated local economic activities to handouts from the refugee agencies or imports.

As a nation in general or state, well thought out and planned blueprints of Mr. Alaak's caliber are needed to address the suspicious and antagonistic relations among the tribes, the lack of qualified and trained professionals especially in education, and over dependence on imports and UN agencies. Policy makers and agencies, who are working with South Sudanese would greatly benefit by adopting and using Mr. Alaak's research work as a basis for visionary strategic planning.

Emmanuel Gai Solomon is a doctoral student at Brenau University, working on educational leadership in Science and Mathematics. He holds master's degree in Instructional Technology from Georgia Southern University and bachelor's degree in Mathematics from the University of the South.

www.ingramcontent.com/pod-product-compliance
Lightning Source LLC
Chambersburg PA
CBHW030302010526
44107CB00053B/1791